BELONGS TO:

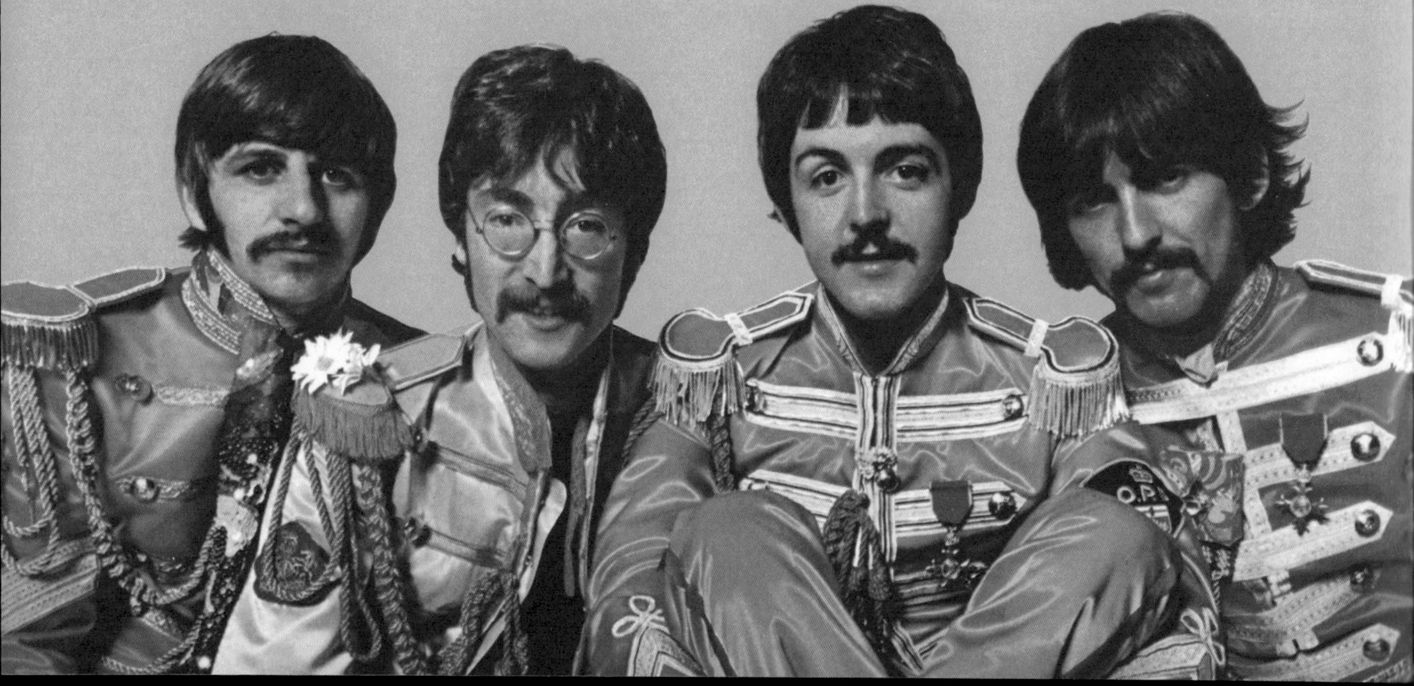

Sgt PEPPERS
LONELY HEARTS
CLUB BAND

Sgt PEPPERS
LONELY HEARTS
CLUB BAND

Sgt PEPPERS
LONELY HEARTS
CLUB BAND

Sgt PEPPERS LONELY HEARTS CLUB BAND

Sgt PEPPERS
LONELY HEARTS
CLUB BAND

Sgt PEPPERS LONELY HEARTS CLUB BAND

Sgt PEPPERS
LONELY HEARTS
CLUB BAND

Sgt PEPPERS
LONELY HEARTS
CLUB BAND

SGT PEPPERS
LONELY HEARTS
CLUB BAND

S^gt PEPPERS LONELY HEARTS CLUB BAND

Sgt PEPPERS LONELY HEARTS CLUB BAND

SGT PEPPERS
LONELY HEARTS
CLUB BAND

Sgt PEPPERS
LONELY HEARTS
CLUB BAND

Sgt PEPPERS LONELY HEARTS CLUB BAND

Sgt PEPPERS LONELY HEARTS CLUB BAND

Sgt PEPPERS LONELY HEARTS CLUB BAND

Sgt PEPPERS
LONELY HEARTS
CLUB BAND

Sgt PEPPERS LONELY HEARTS CLUB BAND

Sgt PEPPERS
LONELY HEARTS
CLUB BAND

Sgt PEPPERS
LONELY HEARTS
CLUB BAND

Sgt PEPPERS LONELY HEARTS CLUB BAND

Sgt PEPPERS LONELY HEARTS CLUB BAND

Sgt PEPPERS
LONELY HEARTS
CLUB BAND

Sgt PEPPERS
LONELY HEARTS
CLUB BAND

Sgt PEPPERS LONELY HEARTS CLUB BAND

Sgt PEPPERS LONELY HEARTS CLUB BAND

SGT PEPPERS
LONELY HEARTS
CLUB BAND

Sgt PEPPERS
LONELY HEARTS
CLUB BAND

Sgt PEPPERS LONELY HEARTS CLUB BAND

Sgt PEPPERS LONELY HEARTS CLUB BAND

Sgt PEPPERS LONELY HEARTS CLUB BAND

Sgt PEPPERS LONELY HEARTS CLUB BAND

Sgt PEPPERS LONELY HEARTS CLUB BAND

Sgt PEPPERS
LONELY HEARTS
CLUB BAND

SGT PEPPERS
LONELY HEARTS
CLUB BAND

Sgt PEPPERS
LONELY HEARTS
CLUB BAND

Sgt PEPPERS LONELY HEARTS CLUB BAND

Sgt PEPPERS LONELY HEARTS CLUB BAND

Sgt PEPPERS LONELY HEARTS CLUB BAND

Sgt PEPPERS LONELY HEARTS CLUB BAND

Sgt PEPPERS LONELY HEARTS CLUB BAND

SGT. PEPPERS
LONELY HEARTS
CLUB BAND

SGT. PEPPERS
LONELY HEARTS
CLUB BAND

Sgt PEPPERS LONELY HEARTS CLUB BAND

Sgt PEPPERS
LONELY HEARTS
CLUB BAND

SGT PEPPERS
LONELY HEARTS
CLUB BAND

SGT PEPPERS
LONELY HEARTS
CLUB BAND

Sgt PEPPERS LONELY HEARTS CLUB BAND

Sgt PEPPERS
LONELY HEARTS
CLUB BAND

SGT PEPPERS
LONELY HEARTS
CLUB BAND

SGT PEPPERS
LONELY HEARTS
CLUB BAND

Sgt PEPPERS
LONELY HEARTS
CLUB BAND

Sgt. PEPPERS LONELY HEARTS CLUB BAND

SGT PEPPERS LONELY HEARTS CLUB BAND

Sgt PEPPERS LONELY HEARTS CLUB BAND

Sgt PEPPERS
LONELY HEARTS
CLUB BAND

SGT. PEPPERS
LONELY HEARTS
CLUB BAND

Sgt PEPPERS
LONELY HEARTS
CLUB BAND

SGT PEPPERS
LONELY HEARTS
CLUB BAND

Sgt PEPPERS LONELY HEARTS CLUB BAND

Sgt PEPPERS LONELY HEARTS CLUB BAND

SGT. PEPPERS LONELY HEARTS CLUB BAND

Sgt PEPPERS LONELY HEARTS CLUB BAND

Sgt PEPPERS LONELY HEARTS CLUB BAND

Sgt PEPPERS
LONELY HEARTS
CLUB BAND

Sgt PEPPERS
LONELY HEARTS
CLUB BAND

S^GT PEPPERS LONELY HEARTS CLUB BAND

Sgt PEPPERS
LONELY HEARTS
CLUB BAND

Sgt PEPPERS LONELY HEARTS CLUB BAND

Sgt PEPPERS
LONELY HEARTS
CLUB BAND

Sgt PEPPERS LONELY HEARTS CLUB BAND

Sgt PEPPERS LONELY HEARTS CLUB BAND

SGT PEPPERS
LONELY HEARTS
CLUB BAND

SGT PEPPERS
LONELY HEARTS
CLUB BAND

Sgt PEPPERS
LONELY HEARTS
CLUB BAND

SGT PEPPERS
LONELY HEARTS
CLUB BAND

Sgt PEPPERS LONELY HEARTS CLUB BAND

SGT PEPPERS
LONELY HEARTS
CLUB BAND

SGT PEPPERS LONELY HEARTS CLUB BAND

Sgt PEPPERS LONELY HEARTS CLUB BAND

SGT. PEPPERS
LONELY HEARTS
CLUB BAND

Sgt PEPPERS
LONELY HEARTS
CLUB BAND

Sgt PEPPERS LONELY HEARTS CLUB BAND

SGT PEPPERS
LONELY HEARTS
CLUB BAND

SGT. PEPPERS LONELY HEARTS CLUB BAND

Sgt PEPPERS
LONELY HEARTS
CLUB BAND

SGT PEPPERS LONELY HEARTS CLUB BAND

Sgt PEPPERS
LONELY HEARTS
CLUB BAND

SGT PEPPERS
LONELY HEARTS
CLUB BAND

Sgt PEPPERS LONELY HEARTS CLUB BAND

SGT. PEPPER'S LONELY HEARTS CLUB BAND

Sgt PEPPERS
LONELY HEARTS
CLUB BAND

SGT PEPPERS LONELY HEARTS CLUB BAND

SGT PEPPERS LONELY HEARTS CLUB BAND

SGT PEPPERS
LONELY HEARTS
CLUB BAND

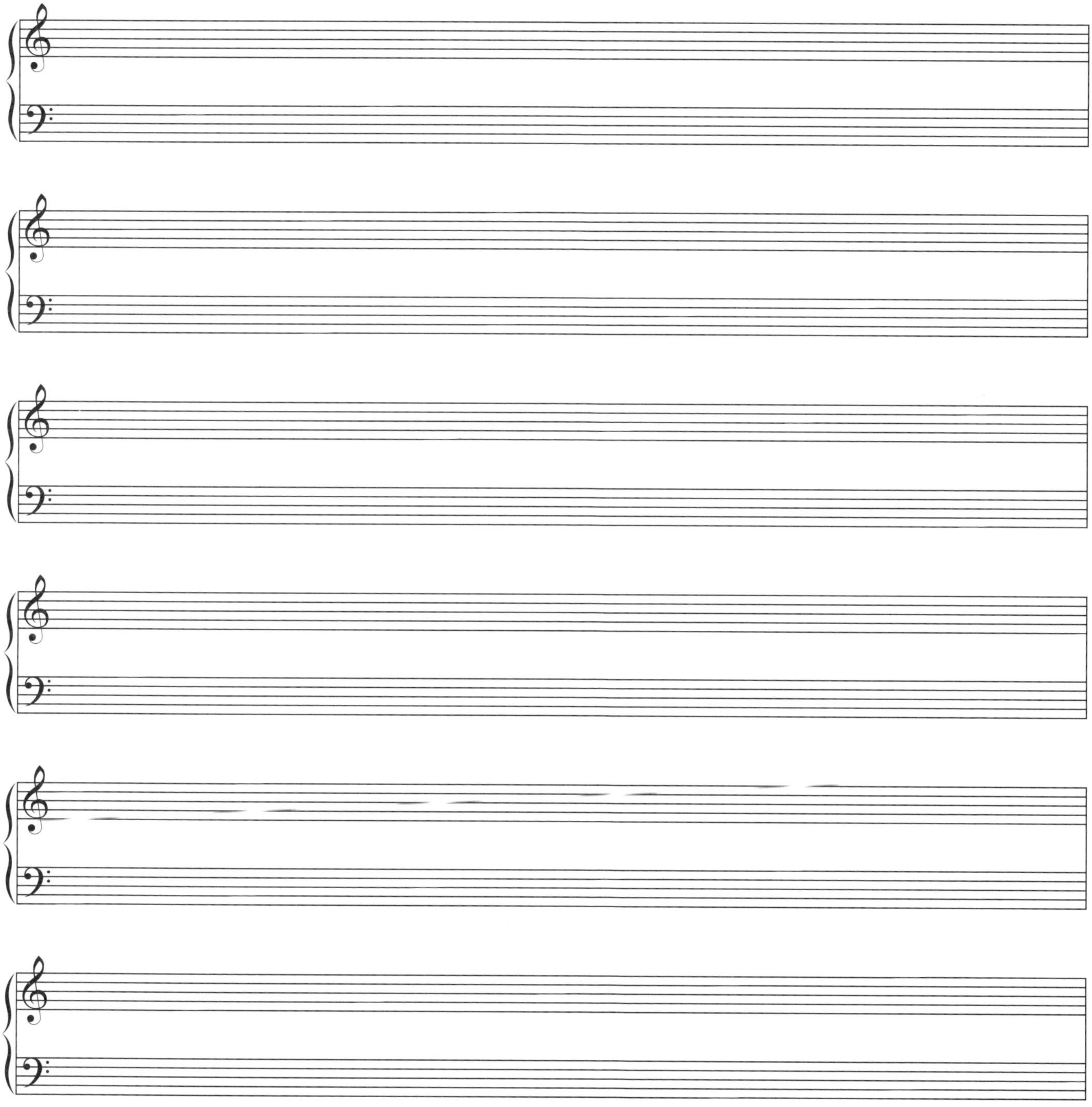

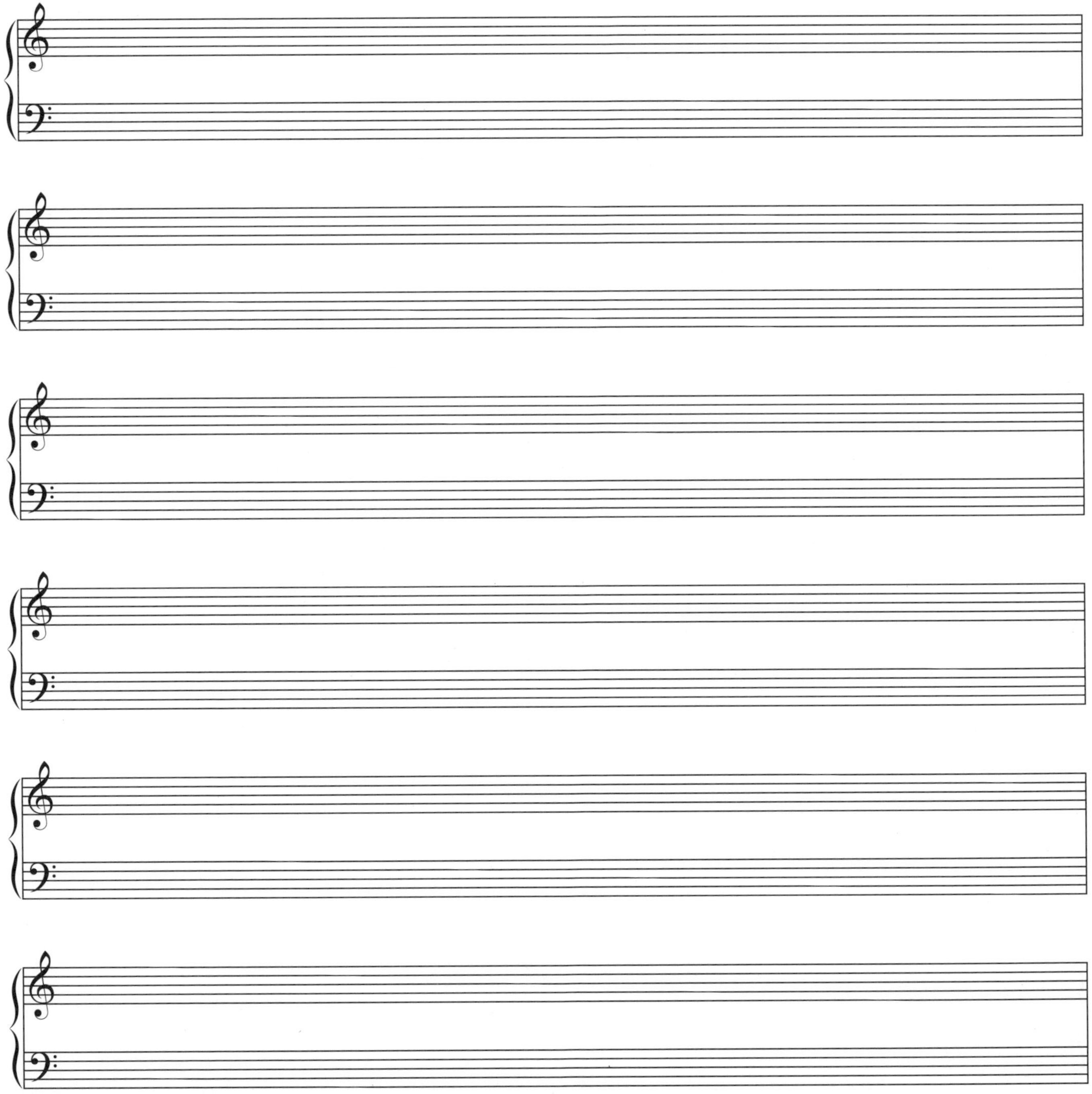

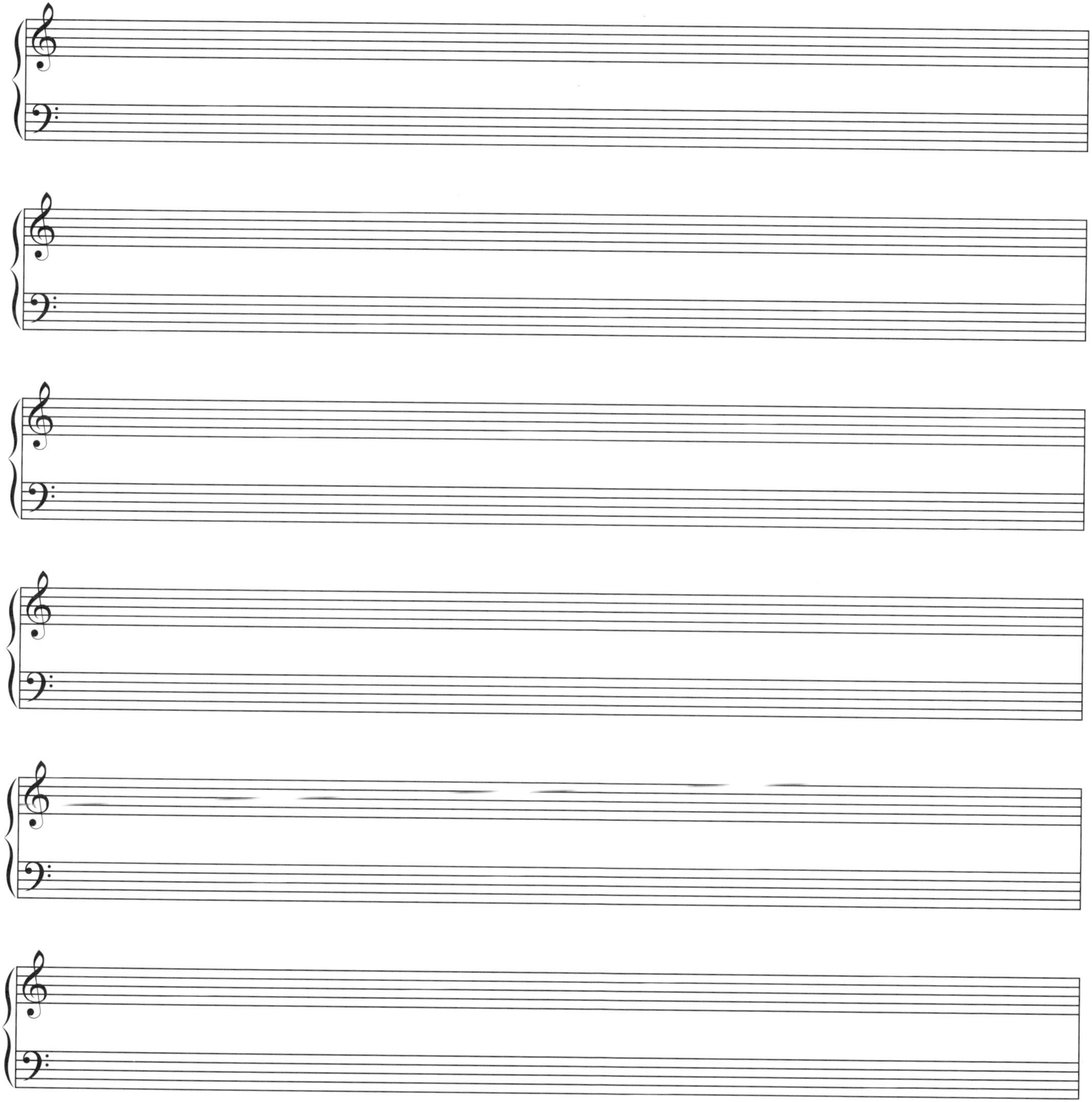

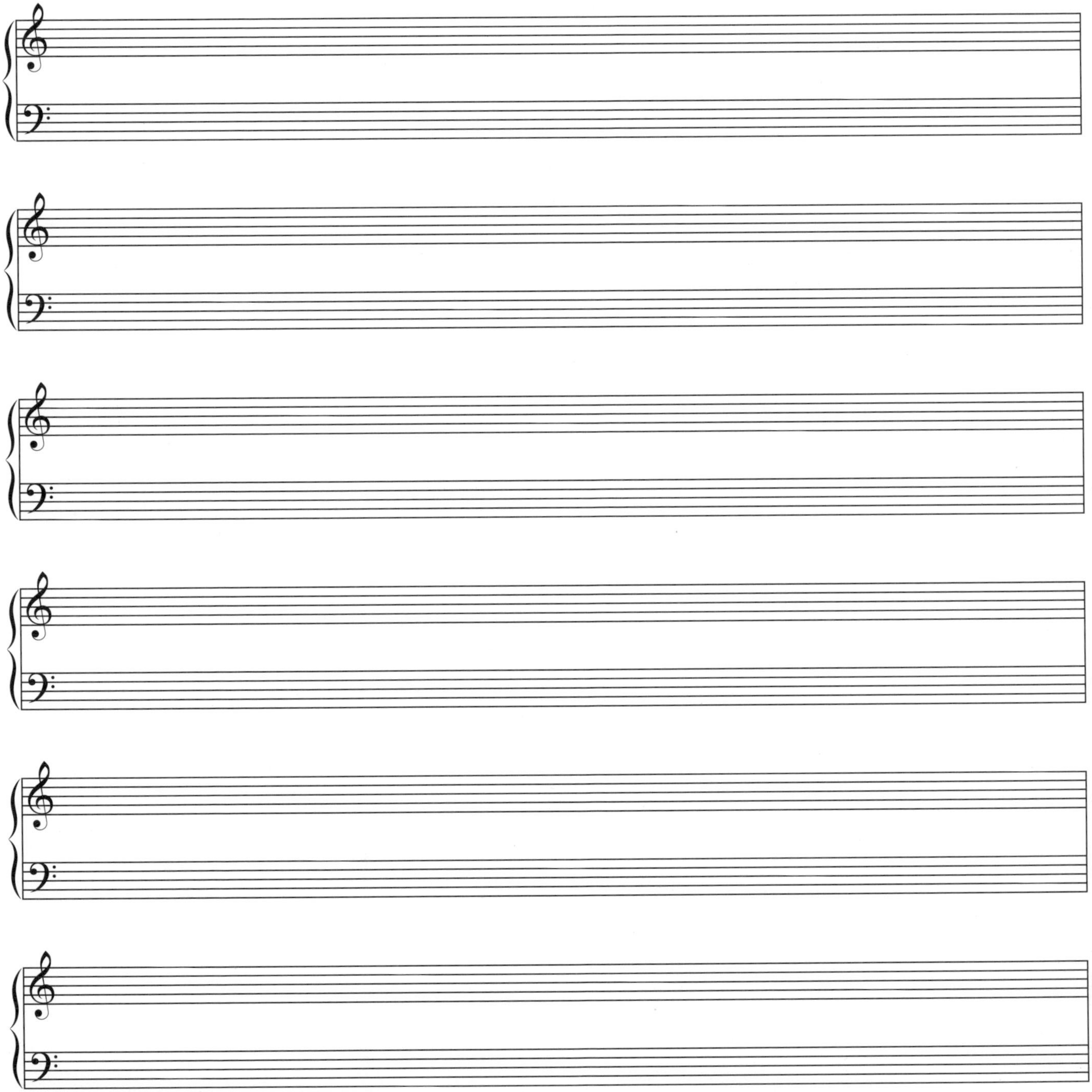

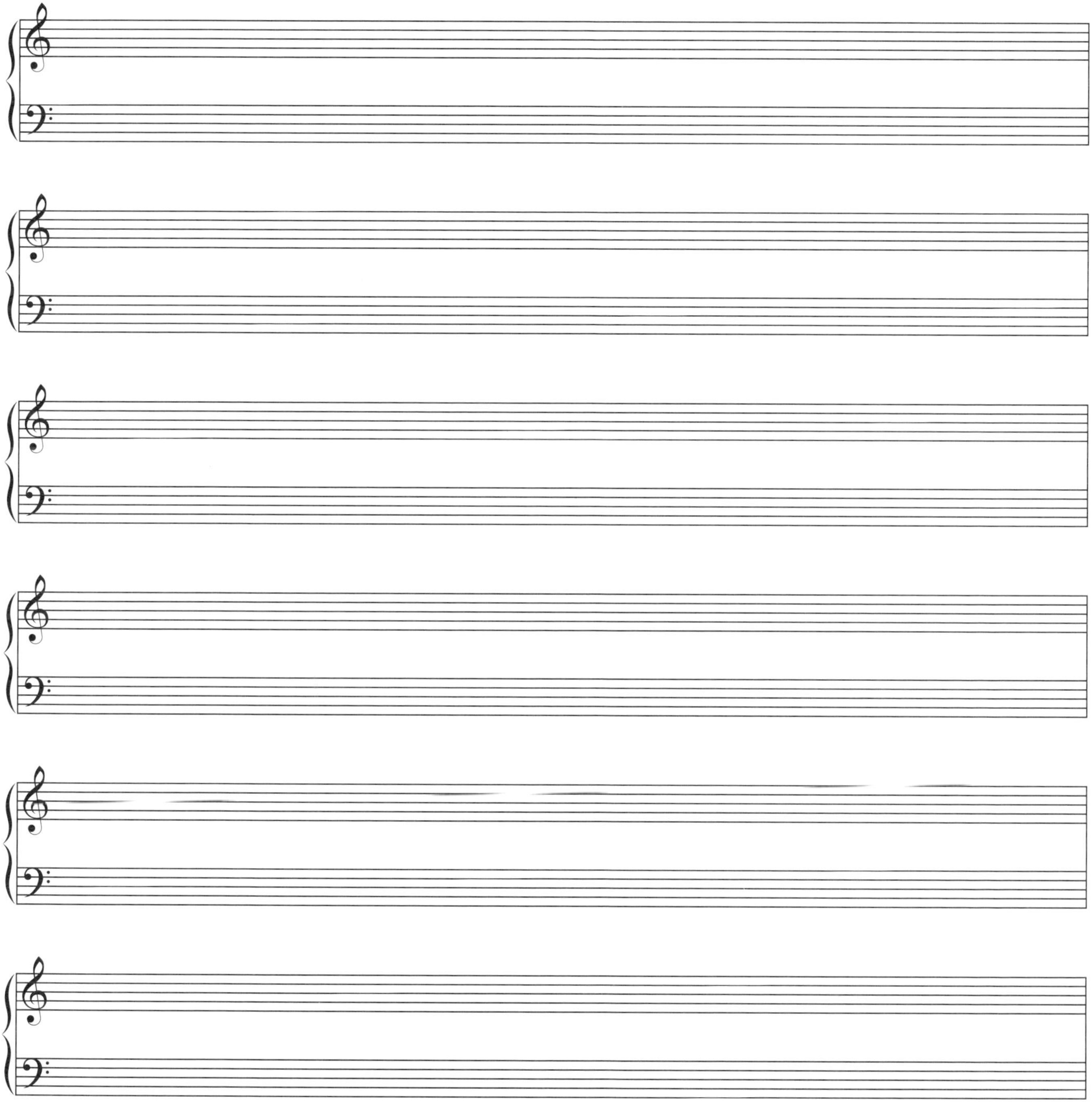

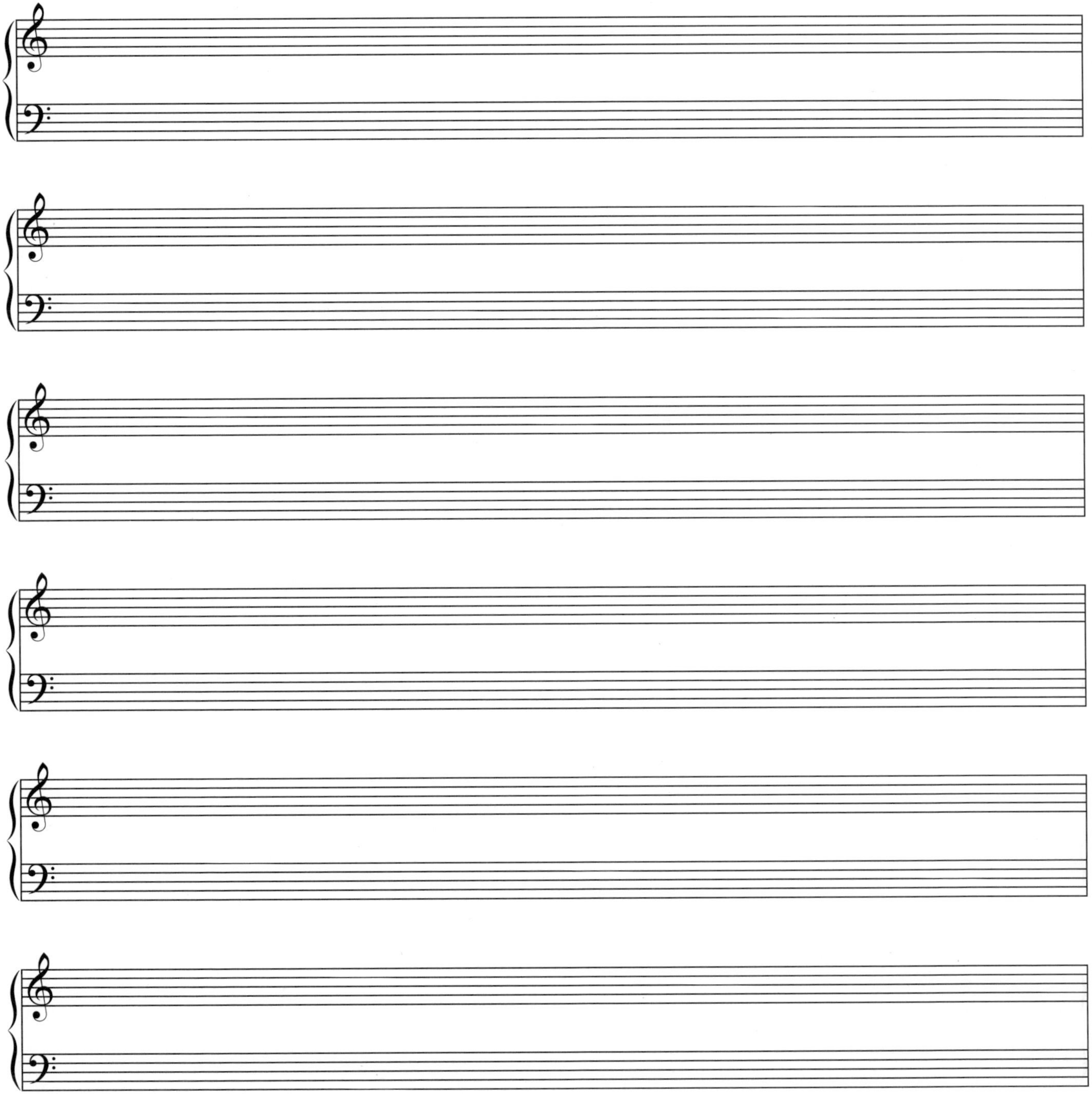